AF585540

The Little Yellow Digger TREASURY

BETTY & ALAN GILDERDALE

SCHOLASTIC
AUCKLAND SYDNEY NEW YORK LONDON TORONTO
MEXICO CITY NEW DELHI HONG KONG

This treasury edition first published in 2025
by Scholastic New Zealand Limited
Private Bag 94407, Botany, Auckland 2163, New Zealand

Scholastic Australia Pty Limited
PO Box 579, Gosford, NSW 2250, Australia

ISBN 978-1-77543-960-8

A catalogue record for this book is available from the National Library of New Zealand.

---

12 11 10 9 8 7 6 5 4 3 2 1 5 6 7 8 9 / 2

Illustrations are watercolour, pen and carbon pencil on paper.

Publishing team: Lynette Evans, Penny Scown and Sophia Broom
Designer: Vida & Luke Kelly Design
Typeset in Bembo
Printed in China by RR Donnelley

Scholastic New Zealand's policy is to use papers that are renewable and made efficiently from wood grown in sustainable forests, so as to minimise its environmental footprint.

A NOTE FROM THE AUTHOR

One dismal, wet August afternoon we were babysitting our two young grandsons in West Auckland. A digger was working in the garden but it stuck in the mud and another digger had to be sent for.

The younger grandson was still having an afternoon rest and when I went to pick him up I heard myself say, "They've brought a bigger digger but the bigger digger's stuck!"

This sounded fun, so that evening I wrote a poem for my grandsons about diggers getting stuck in the mud. I read it to them over the phone the next day with the result that for the next week they were ringing me up two or three times daily, saying, "Please Gran, tell us the story of the diggers."

At the time, I had no intention of writing a picture book story but it did seem as though my market research had already been done! I suggested to my husband, Alan, a talented artist and lecturer in art, that we should make the digger story into a picture book. His reply was definite. "I am not going to draw diggers," he said.

He needed some persuasion, but by the end of a week, after I had persisted with the picture book idea, he finally said, "Oh, all right!"

The first edition of *The Little Yellow Digger* came out in 1993 and it has been continuously in print ever since. It has given us great pleasure and kept us in touch with children whenever we visited schools.

—*Betty Gilderdale*

CONTENTS

The Little Yellow Digger

BETTY & ALAN GILDERDALE

In the next door garden
they were digging out a drain
when the weather turned quite nasty
and it poured and poured with rain.

The garden got so muddy
that the little digger stuck,

so they sent another digger
and it really was bad luck

that it slid upon the mud
in the wind and the rain,
and fell upon its side
in the half-dug drain.

So they got a bigger digger,
but the bigger digger stuck,

then a bigger **bigger** digger
was brought up on a truck.
It was huge and it was heavy
and – you guessed it –

it got STUCK!

Now in the next door garden,
slowly sinking in the ground,
was the little yellow digger
with its wheels spinning round,
and a digger on its side
in the half-dug drain,
with the bigger red digger
(which had ropes and a chain)

and the bigger **bigger** digger,
all shining in the rain.
They were sunk down deep
with the bright red truck.
Deep down in the mud...

and all of them STUCK!

Then the drivers had a meeting
and they said they wouldn't stay,
but promised they'd come back
when the rain had gone away.

And only two days later
the wind blew brisk and dry,
and the sun shone very brightly
from a blue and cloudless sky.

The mud dried hard as concrete,
so when the men came back,
the bigger **bigger** digger
was still stuck upon the track.

They couldn't make its engine
turn the wheels around.
The mud had hardened round it
and trapped it in the ground.

Mud trapped the bigger digger
with its ropes and its chain
so it couldn't pull the digger
from the half-dug drain.

But the little yellow digger
was standing on firm ground.
They managed now to start it,
and the wheels turned around.

It was the little yellow digger
that pulled the digger from the drain...

and they both together pulled
the bigger digger with its chain.

Then all three pulled **together** ...

till with a clatter and a thud
the bigger **bigger** digger
rumbled up out of the mud.

So the bigger **bigger** digger
and its truck went back,
and they drove the other diggers
home along the track.

But the little yellow digger
stayed to finish off the drain.
It helped to make a driveway
that would stay hard in the rain.

And often we remember
those diggers and the truck…

and how it rained…

and all the mud…

and everything
got STUCK!

The Little Yellow Digger and the Bones

BETTY & ALAN GILDERDALE

It started to rain on the Monday,
it rained on the Tuesday as well,
it bucketed down on the Wednesday,
and rivers were starting to swell.

There was thunder and lightning on Thursday,
bridges and roads swept away.

By Friday the hillsides had crumbled,
and traffic was held up all day.

Where bushes and boulders had tumbled,
diggers were needed to clear them away.

There were diggers of all shapes and sizes,
a back hoe with big grapple teeth . . .

a loader with huge scraper buckets,
and tough crawler tyres underneath.

A little yellow digger came last
to help where a cave had appeared.
The digger was small, so could reach it.
With caution, a way could be cleared.

Whatever might be inside it?
It might be like stories of old —
where fierce, fire-breathing dragons
guarded treasure of rubies and gold.

The digger was clearing the rubble
– boulders and thick, sticky mud –
when, all of a sudden, the driver
felt a shudder and heard a great THUD!

He climbed from the cab very quickly.
He wondered if they'd struck a stone,
but found that it was a very large rock
and from it was poking a bone!

The bone was simply enormous;
too big for a horse or a cow.
It must have been there many ages,
locked in the rock until now.

Inside the cave there were fragments
of what looked like very large teeth,
and more rocks with bones showing in them
as he carefully dug underneath.

He rang the Museum to help them;
they answered the call straight away.

Two people came out to take photos
and measure the bones where they lay.

What animal had the bones come from?
And how long had they been there?

They needed more experts to tell them,
so they lifted the rocks with great care.

The digger had now cleared a pathway
so their van could get out with its load.
The rocks had been packed very gently –
they must not be harmed on the road.

Their colours were no longer shiny:
the back hoe (with big grapple teeth)
was dirty, and so was the loader,
its crawler tyres muddy beneath.

The little yellow digger went last,
as its driver had stayed to make sure
that the cave had been boarded up safely,
its rocks and its bones all secure.

It was not until many months later,
after the flood and the rain,
a notice appeared in the paper,
recalling the story again:

★NEWS★

EXCITING FIND BY LITTLE YELLOW DIGGER!

When a little yellow digger was clearing away mud and rubble after last year's floods, some strange bones were discovered.

The very same day came a letter;
the driver undid it with care.
Inside was a grand invitation
to a party to meet with the Mayor.

The party was at the Museum,
it must be a special event.
People were very excited –
television had even been sent!

Indoors, the Mayor was waiting near a curtain that fully concealed whatever it was the digger had found, which was now to be revealed!

It was A DINOSAUR!

There were the bones,
there were the teeth,
there was the head
and, written beneath:

This is a THERAPOD,
a dinosaur that was
a carnivore. It liked its
meat, and that's why
it had so many teeth!

Then everyone thanked the digger
for the work it had done in the flood,
and praises were heaped on its driver
for finding the bone in the mud.

The Little Yellow Digger at the Zoo

BETTY & ALAN GILDERDALE

"Too many hippos," the chief keeper said,
as he took off his cap and he scratched his bald head.
"I'm afraid that a number may soon have to go."

But the keeper's assistant quite loudly said, "No!
Too many hippos? Oh no, not at all.
It's the pool that's the problem; it's really too small.
All that we need is to get in a digger
to come and to dig and to make the hole bigger."

The little yellow digger arrived the next day,
and the keepers then took all the hippos away.

They were taken along to the sea lions' pool.

It was rather a squash, but it kept them all cool.

Then the hippos' pool was drained quite dry
and the water sank with a glug and a sigh.

The little yellow digger was really quite small
but it started at once to break down the wall,
and it worked very hard with a *clatter-thump-thud*
to dig very deeply down into the mud.

The digger dug deep and the digger dug wide …

till the hole grew so big that it vanished inside.

Then up from below came a worrying shout,

But the keeper said crossly, "I very much doubt
we can find a big digger to haul you both out.
There's not enough room around the edge of the pool
for a digger that's bigger to give you a pull."

But a clever young girl who was standing nearby shouted, "How about letting an elephant try?"

And the keeper replied, "That's a splendid idea. Send for the elephant – we need it here."

So the elephant came with a thumpety-thump.
It was flapping its ears and swinging its trunk.

Then they harnessed it up and they threw a rope down to the driver, who caught it and wound it around.

He made loops and some knots that he pulled very tight.
"That's done it," he shouted. "We'll soon be all right."

Then the elephant gave a strong tug and a pull
and slowly, from out of the wide, empty pool,

the digger appeared, but what very bad luck!

It slipped over sideways and ended up STUCK!

The keeper's assistant said, "Leave it to me.
We'll fix up a pulley by using that tree."

He cautiously clambered along the tree bough
and tossed down the rope to the keeper, who now
tied it onto the elephant so it could pull
that small digger upwards and out of the pool.

Could that be the answer? Oh no! Not at all!
The digger was swinging, it seemed it would fall.
It was swaying and dangling high up in the air.
"It's no good!" they all cried. "It just *can't* be left there."

"We need a strong animal on the far side
to pull it right over," the cross keeper cried,
"but we've no other elephant left in the shed."

"Well, bring out a camel," the clever girl said.

So they brought out the camel, which wrinkled its nose
as it snuffled and snorted and dug in its toes.
But in spite of the fact that its temper was short,
it was tied with a rope that was then made quite taut.

"Now PULL!" yelled the keeper.
He shouted, "Heave HO!"

And the camel was gently persuaded to go.
It tugged on the rope – but the digger still hung
over the hole, where it teetered and swung.

But at last it was down and they all crowded round
and the driver climbed up onto firm concrete ground.

Then they filled up the pool, now much wider and bigger,

and the elephant washed all the mud off the digger.

Then it squirted the keeper, the cross camel too,

on the day that the digger came out to the zoo.

The Little Yellow Digger Goes to School

BETTY & ALAN GILDERDALE

The little yellow digger
was coming to our school.
The principal had asked it
to dig a swimming pool.

It clattered through the playground.
It came at morning tea.

The driver smiled, “Good morning!”
as we ran around to see.

The bell was ringing loudly.
We had to go to class.
The digger chugged across the field
to dig beneath the grass.

MATHS
WORK SHEET

We crowded round the windows
to see what we could see,
as it began to make a hole
where the pool would be.

Our principal went out to look
(his name was Mr Lane) …

but then the digger hit a pipe
and burst the water main!

A fountain spurted upwards.
It was a water spout!
Then it cascaded downwards …
the driver yelled, "Look out!"

Poor Mr Lane was knocked down flat,
and soaking wet, right through.
"Look what you've done!" he shouted.
"Whatever can we do?"

The water went on gushing
with a swooshing, swishing sound.
It quickly made great puddles
on the muddy football ground.

Just then another teacher
rushed out to lend a hand.
He slipped and slithered on the mud.
He couldn't even stand!

The office phoned the Council:
"Come quickly as you can!"

It wasn't very long before
they sent a helpful man.

ABC 2

He stopped the gushing fountain
once the hydrant had been found,
but said there'd be no water
in the buildings all around.

“The bathrooms will be out of use,”
said worried Mr Lane.

"I know! We'll picnic on the beach
until they've fixed the main."

Just then the Council truck arrived,
the men unpacked their load,
but we'd fetched hats and lunches
and were marching down the road.

Then, while we picnicked on the beach,
the digger worked again
to help the council workmen
repair the broken main.

When we returned at three o'clock,
the water was back on.

The digger was still working.
The men and truck had gone.

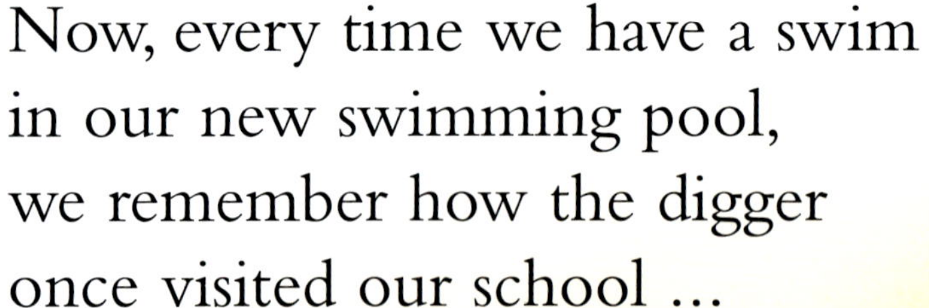

Now, every time we have a swim
in our new swimming pool,
we remember how the digger
once visited our school ...

the unexpected picnic ...

a muddy Mr Lane ...

we do so hope the digger
will come to school again!

The Little Yellow Digger Saves the Whale

BETTY & ALAN GILDERDALE

Rolling and leaping at their play,
two whales swam in a sunlit bay.

The tide was turning quickly,
the mother felt it go,
and straight away swam out to sea.
The baby was too slow.

And now it lay there gasping
in the growing heat of day,
while its very worried mother
swam up and down the bay.

But the little yellow digger
was not very far inland.
Its driver had a message
to go and lend a hand.

They rattled down the rocky road
that led towards the sea.
The little whale was stranded there.
They'd help to set it free.

The digger drove between the rocks
in the early morning sun.
Its driver looked about him
to see what could be done.

He would have to dig a channel,
deep enough and wide,
to float the little whale out
upon the turning tide.

The whale's home was water.
Its skin must not be dry.
In sunshine it would overheat
and very soon might die.

But people started to arrive
for a picnic by the sea.
Could they keep the whale alive
until it was set free?

Children digging in the sand
were asked to lend a pail,
which they could fill with water
to pour upon the whale.

The digger's driver promised,
if they'd also lend a spade,
he'd help them build a castle
when the whale had been saved.

So while the digger shovelled sand
they organised a team,
of young and old, of tall and small,
to get water from the stream.

Then everybody took a turn
to fill buckets from a pool,
and pass them on along the line
to keep the whale cool.

As they poured the water on the whale just seemed to know that they were trying to help it as they talked and called it "Joe."

And all the while the little digger
dug deep to make the channel bigger.

Every time its shovel filled,
it chugged along the shore,

then emptied it to make a mound
. . . and still it went for more.

The digger now had dug a trench,
deep enough and wide,
to float the little whale out
upon the turning tide.

But the very last few metres
must be dug by spade,
because the digger's clatter
would make the whale afraid.

The time had come,
the tide had turned.

The waves surged in,
the whale could swim.

Right out it went,
in sea and spray,
to join its mother in the bay.

Then everybody raised a cheer
for the driver and the digger
because they set the whale free
when they made the channel bigger.

"Now pick up buckets, pick up spades!"
the digger's driver said.
"We'll make a castle from that mound
before we go to bed."

They patted, dug and shaped the mound
till on that sunny day,
the biggest castle ever made
stood in the tree-fringed bay.

While rolling, leaping at their play,
two whales swam in the sunlit bay.